ARCTIC
TALE

Arctic Tale has been created from the best Arctic wildlife cinematography of the past decade. Nanu and Seela are composite characters whose lives are based upon material shot throughout the Arctic over many years. Their stories represent the real conditions polar bears and walruses face today.

The events, characters, entities and/or firms depicted in this motion picture and book are fictitious. Any similarity to actual events or persons, living or dead, or to actual entities or firms is purely coincidental.

Library of Congress Cataloging-in-Publication Data
Fifield, Donnali.
Arctic Tale / adapted by Donnali Fifield.
    p. cm.
 "Narration Written by Linda Woolverton and Mose Richards and Kristin Gore."
 ISBN 978-1-4262-0065-6
 1. Walrus—Arctic regions. 2. Polar bear—Arctic regions. 3. Wildlife photography—Arctic regions. I. Ravetch, Adam. II. Robertson, Sarah. III. Title.
QL737.P62F54 2007
599.79'909113—dc22   2007008770

Founded in 1888, the National Geographic Society is one of the largest nonprofit scientific and educational organizations in the world. It reaches more than 285 million people worldwide each month through its official journal, NATIONAL GEOGRAPHIC, and its four other magazines; the National Geographic Channel; television documentaries; radio programs; films; books; videos and DVDs; maps; and interactive media. National Geographic has funded more than 8,000 scientific research projects and supports an education program combating geographic illiteracy.

For more information, please call
1-800-NGS LINE (647-5463)
or write to the following address:

National Geographic Society
1145 17th Street N.W.
Washington, D.C. 20036-4688 U.S.A.

Visit us online at
www.nationalgeographic.com/books

For information about special discounts for bulk purchases, please contact
National Geographic Books Special Sales:
ngspecsales@ngs.org

For rights or permissions inquiries, please contact
National Geographic Books Subsidiary Rights:
ngbookrights@ngs.org

Printed in U.S.A.

ARCTIC TALE

Narration Written by Linda Woolverton
and Mose Richards and Kristin Gore
Adapted by Donnali Fifield

NATIONAL GEOGRAPHIC

WASHINGTON, D.C.

CONTENTS

A polar bear stretches out on the ice for a nap.
PAGES 6-7: *Diving underwater, a walrus heads toward the seafloor to feed.*
PAGES 8-9: *Aerial view off the coast of Little Diomede Island, Alaska.*
PAGES 10-11: *A sandbar divides the Chukchi Sea, at left, from Kasegaluk Lagoon. The sea lies between Alaska and Russia.*

FOREWORD

WHEN WE FIRST WENT INTO THE ARCTIC MORE THAN 15 YEARS AGO, WE KNEW IMMEDIATELY that we had found something unique and alien. Between us, we had already explored a third of the globe, diving and filming in oceans throughout the world. But neither of us had ever felt as riveted by a region as we were by the north.

The Arctic kept calling us in compelling ways. Its sharp, icy world gleamed in the light like a cut jewel enchanting us with its raw beauty. Its powerful and unpredictable weather constantly challenged us. The mysteries of its wildlife and their struggle for survival fascinated us. Its incongruities, where cold is good and hot is bad, perplexed us and made us think in new ways.

Most of all, though, we were attracted to the sense of continuity and connection in the Arctic. Everything in the north is contained and accumulated in an ancient well of knowledge. Unlike most humans, northern people and animals live in extreme cold, in a polar desert where almost nothing grows. Survival in these harsh conditions requires remarkable life strategies—strategies that have been discovered over time through watching, learning, trying, and perfecting. Once learned, they are strictly followed, and the reward is survival.

The Inuit of the north learned from watching polar bears how to hunt seals through ice holes. This technique is still used today and is an example of the continuity of unbroken knowledge followed rigorously in order to survive.

The Arctic is a place where the biological diversity of life is limited. Only a few species have learned to live in this environment, and life truly is linked and interdependent. In such a place the continuity of knowledge can be felt very strongly, and it commanded in us a deep respect and admiration.

Our filming experiences in the north involved the good fortune and timing to consult and to travel with some of the last of the old, traditional Inuit hunters. These people had a very strong connection to the Arctic landscape and its animals. They saw things that we could not see, and they guided us through truly amazing feats of survival. We have them to thank for many of the images in *Arctic Tale* and for instilling in us a love for the north. Most of these great hunters are gone now, but to this day we continue to work with their sons and daughters.

A great deal of our work centered on the walrus and the polar bear. These two animals—which seemed so big, frightening, and unapproachable—were much more than that. We learned that both bears and walruses have strong parental bonds—a commitment of up to three years by the females in both species for raising their young. The day we witnessed the dedication and the teachings that a mother walrus displayed toward her calf was a revelation. The emotion of it hit us strongly. We recognized ourselves, our humanity, our mammalian way of teaching, and the continuity of knowledge being passed from mother to calf.

But what happens to such a place, where continuity and traditional knowledge is so important, when conditions start changing? In the Arctic, we have seen the seasonal patterns of the ice's thaw and freeze shift dramatically. The glaciers are shrinking and, each year, the ice is taking longer to reform. The landscape is transforming and, as a result, the walruses and bears have been forced to change their own ways of hunting and surviving. But will it be enough?

How will the Inuit people and the animals change? What will happen to the ancient Arctic knowledge? How will this affect the rest of the world?

As filmmakers, we are honored to have been able to make this film of the Arctic. We want to thank all the people who helped us assemble these precious images, a photographic record of our heritage in the North. It captures a place that many humans will never see—a world that is rapidly changing and that deserves to be remembered.

—Adam Ravetch and Sarah Robertson

Midnight sun over the Norwegian island of Senja and its fjords.

Chapter One

THE ICE KINGDOM

a cross the northern seas, at the top of the world, lies an immense and abundant kingdom. To most of us, the Arctic seems a frozen wasteland. But to the creatures that have adapted to its astonishing cold, its vast expanses of ice are a paradise.

This is the tale of two newborns, from birth to adulthood. Their story begins in spring, when the sun starts to warm the Arctic.

Born a few months apart, Nanu, a polar bear cub, and Seela, a walrus calf, discover their world at the same time. They are alike in other ways, too. Their species are among the giants of the Arctic. Both are descended from land mammals. To find food, their ancestors became adept in the water and on the ice, moving from the land to the sea. And each has a highly devoted mother. This is the most intimate link between them, and the most critical to their survival in this harsh environment.

For the next few years, their mothers will teach them how to endure the cold, how to hunt, and how to recognize danger—skills passed down through generation after generation of walrus and polar bear mothers. After evolving for tens of thousands of years to thrive in this universe of snow and ice, walruses, polar bears, and the other animals that have made their home here must now adjust to their rapidly changing world. Temperatures in the Arctic are increasing twice as fast as anywhere else on Earth.

Sea ice at the shore of Kiatak Island, Greenland, seen from a helicopter.

Lying on an ice floe, a walrus mother keeps an eye on her newborn at all times. A female walrus will risk her life to save her calf.

Nanuq means "polar bear" in the Inuit language, but can have different spellings in the various dialects of the Inuit.
FOLLOWING PAGES: *Beneath the Arctic's pack ice lie clam beds where walruses forage for food. After eating, they haul out on the ice to rest.*

Called whitecoats by seal hunters, harp seal newborns shed their thick lanugo coat by the time they are weaned. As they mature, they develop a black, harp-shaped pattern on their back. OPPOSITE: *Arctic fox kits emerge from their den about three weeks after birth. Litter size ranges from 7 to 12 depending on the abundance of food and other factors.*

Mostly frozen ocean, the Arctic is ringed by islands and by North America, Europe, and Asia. The Arctic connects to the Pacific through the Bering Strait and to the Atlantic primarily through the Greenland Sea—an area so wide that the floating ice cap at its center is about the size of the contiguous United States. The polar cap remains frozen throughout the year. But along the coasts that surround the ocean, the ice melts, breaks up, and reforms each year. Every spring, the ice begins to recede. Every fall, the shore ices over again. The annual rhythm of the ice sustains a profusion of wildlife, including migratory birds and whales that return north to feed as the ice clears. Now, though, the ice is shrinking, disrupting this cycle and affecting every species, from the tiniest plankton to the massive bowhead whales.

Chapter Two

EARLY SPRING

Like all newborns, Nanu and Seela have much to learn. But to rear them, their mothers will not only have to protect them from predators, blizzards, and the other traditional threats of the Arctic, they will have to adapt to the changing conditions in the North.

In early spring, miles of ice still separate the shore from the open sea. Made of frozen ocean, the ice stretches from the snow-covered mountains on the coast to the floe edge, the boundary between the ice and the sea. High up in the mountains, a polar bear has given birth to two cubs. Born in the darkness of winter, the cubs could not see or hear at birth, and weighed only a little more than a pound. They had almost no fur to protect them from the weather outside. In the warmth of the den, the cubs have developed fur and have grown to nearly 30 pounds (14 kg), nursing on their mother's rich milk. Now three months old, Nanu and her twin brother are big enough to leave the den for the first time.

Their mother pokes her nose out of the den—a black spot in a blanket of white. She has been secluded in the den since fall. She checks that all is safe, then climbs out of the den. Sliding on the snow, she grooms herself, cleaning her fur.

Icebergs drift across the water off the coast of Greenland.

Young cubs stay close to their mother for warmth. During their first months, cubs have too little blubber to protect them completely from the cold.

After resting, the polar bear begins to roll around on the snow, using it to clean her fur and groom herself.

Born in November or December, cubs stay in the maternity den until late March or April. A short walk helps acclimate them to traveling on the snow and ice. OPPOSITE: *A cub emerges from the warmth and darkness of the den into the brisk air outside. Despite the sunshine, temperatures remain below freezing.*

The cubs hang back. They look out from the entrance of the den, hesitant to leave the safety of their home. Making a chuffing sound, their mother calls out to them. The cubs run downhill to join her, wrestling as they go. Reassured by being near her, Nanu turns around and heads back up the slope. Her brother follows. But, a little timid, he stays by their mother's side a few seconds longer. They can only stay out of the den a short time, as they are not yet used to the piercing cold. The temperature is 20 degrees below zero (-29°C). Life in the Arctic is so demanding that polar bear cubs typically spend two to three years with their mother learning survival skills. Tomorrow, their mother will take them out again to begin their lessons. Before they can travel down to the sea, they will need more time to adjust to the cold.

Intensely social, walruses congregate in the shallow coastal waters of the Arctic, hauling out on land or ice. A herd can consist of hundreds of members.

One of the most devoted of all mammal mothers, a walrus nuzzles her newborn calf. Walrus mothers also use their front flippers to touch and reassure their young.

The sea ice extends for 30 miles (48 km) from the shore. Just beyond lies a maze of ice floes, where walrus mothers can care for their young away from the rest of the herd. Born just hours ago, Seela explores her world for the first time. Her mother gave birth to her on an ice floe and has led her into the water for her first swim. Although Seela will spend two-thirds of her life in the sea, she was not born knowing how to swim instinctively.

Seela also has to learn how to haul herself out of the water—and she has to learn it soon, or she could get too cold and drown. Like Nanu, she is still vulnerable to the cold.

Her mother holds Seela tenderly with her front flippers. They nuzzle, whisker to whisker. These bristles, called vibrissae, have nerves that make them highly sensitive. The touch of their whiskers helps Seela and her mother become familiar with each other's faces. As they rub muzzles, her mother breathes in her scent. Now, her mother can identify her not only by touch, but also by smell.

Seela barks. When they join the herd, her mother will be able to distinguish her voice amid all the growls, snorts, and grunts. Although Seela is still small, her voice carries as far away as a mile or more.

Protective of the young in their herd, adult walruses respond to the sound of a calf's voice. Some distance away, several walruses look up from the water. Seela's bark draws the attention of a young female. She barks back, and swims toward Seela and her mother. A walrus mother often has a helper, in this case an apprentice learning how to be a mother. Sometimes this nanny walrus is an older sibling of the newborn. The young female does not yet have a baby of her own, so she is free to help take care of Seela. In the coming years, she will serve as the calf's constant protector, taking on an auntlike role. Muzzle to muzzle, they use their mustaches to greet and identify each other.

As her aunt keeps watch for predators, her mother shows her how to haul out onto an ice floe. But Seela would rather turn somersaults in the water. Her mother nudges her up the ice. Using her flippers, Seela lifts herself up. She slides back down again. Another try. She scrambles up higher on the ice. For every accomplishment, her mother rewards her with a flipper hug or a nuzzle.

Polar bears are largely solitary as adults. While a polar bear mother raises her cubs by herself, a walrus mother has her herd to help watch over her young.

Struggling up an ice floe, a calf raises herself on the ice with her flippers. A newborn walrus calf typically weighs about 90 to 150 pounds (41–68 kg).

When the calf's tusks come in, she will be able to hook them into the ice to rest or to pull herself up. OPPOSITE: **Odobenus**, *the genus name for walruses, derives from the Greek words for "tooth walker"—a description of how walruses look as they wield their tusks like pickaxes.*

DOWN
TO THE SEA

each day for the past week, the polar bears have gone outside for a longer and longer period of time. For the cubs, these excursions give them a chance to play. But as they roll in the snow, wrestle, run and tumble, they are building up their muscles and getting used to the cold. They are now ready to leave the den. Their mother has not eaten since last fall. To nurse her cubs, she needs food. The cubs must venture with her down to the frozen ocean, where she can catch ringed seals. And so they leave behind their home to begin the wandering life of polar bears.

Leading the way, she walks down the mountain and across the snowy ice field that stretches out to the floe edge. The Inuit call this procession *atiqtuq,* bears going down to the sea. Nanu and her brother follow so close behind their mother that they are underfoot. She walks carefully, lifting her legs around them.

An arctic fox tags along, shadowing them to nab a bite from any prey she might catch. Arctic foxes often follow bears to scavenge from their kills.

Walking on the ice behind Nanu's family, the fox is well protected from the cold. He has a dense white coat, which provides excellent insulation. When he lies down to rest, he can wrap his long tail around his face for extra warmth.

Bylot Island in Canada serves as a polar bear denning area.

After digging a temporary den in the snow, a polar bear stops to let her cubs nurse and rest. Ptarmigans stand on nearby snowdrifts.

A cub climbs on his mother's back. A polar bear mother occasionally carries her cubs on her back while crossing water or going through thick snow.

Like polar bears, arctic foxes hunt ringed seal pups, and they also scavenge, following the bears to snatch from their kills.

As she walks, Nanu's mother smells for seals beneath the ice. Polar bears primarily feed on ringed seals. They hunt the seals at their breathing holes, when the seals haul out on the ice. In the spring, the bears also stalk the seals' pups. Like walruses, ringed seals give birth in spring. Their plump pups are almost half fat, which provides the bears with quick energy. The fox hunts the seal pups, too. He prefers lemmings, but will eat whatever comes his way, including voles, birds, eggs, and berries.

In the snow, Nanu's mother comes upon the paw prints of the only animal in the Ice Kingdom she needs to fear. A male bear is up ahead in the distance. She stops. He might attack her cubs. Male bears sometimes kill cubs for food or to mate with their mother. She makes a chuffing noise to warn her cubs, then runs, checking to make sure that they are following her. But the male, standing on his hind legs and sniffing the air, is more interested in a scent he has detected in the wind: Seela.

Smelling a ringed seal lair from more than a mile away, an arctic fox rises up, then pounds on the ice to break through the lair roof and grab the seal pup. Adult foxes weigh only 6 to 12 pounds (3–6 kg).

The cubs' claws, as well as the hair and tiny bumps on the bottom of their feet, give them traction as they follow their mother across the frozen sea.

Polar bears have large, partially webbed front paws. Moving swiftly through the water, they use their back paws like rudders.
OPPOSITE: *The polar bears' scientific name is **Ursus maritimus**, or "sea bear." Their nostrils close while they are underwater, where they swim at depths of up to 15 feet (4.5 m).*

After a swim, polar bears shake the water and ice from their fur, then frequently crawl in the snow to dry off.

A walrus can dive to a depth of 300 feet (90 m). OPPOSITE: *Walruses use their tusks to fend off attacks. The size of their tusks also indicates their age and sex, determining their status with other walruses. Large walruses with long, unbroken tusks are the most dominant members of the herd.*

The bear can smell prey that is 20 miles (32 km) away. Seela and her mother are miles from him, resting on an ice floe. He slides into the water and swims toward them.

Seela's aunt spots the bear. She barks to give warning. Seela's mother prods Seela into the sea, then dives in behind her. Clutching Seela with her flippers, she swims away. The bear's webbed paws help make him a strong swimmer. His average swimming speed is about 6 miles an hour (10 km/h)—two miles an hour faster than hers. He can catch them. But bears rely on sea ice as a platform to help them hunt. Although they can sometimes capture prey in the open water, they are not effective hunters in the sea. And at 1,300 pounds (600 kg) or more, nearly twice his weight, Seela's aunt is a powerful opponent. She races to block him, planting herself between the bear and Seela and her mother. She jabs at him with her tusks. He quickly gives up. He hunts young walruses, whose tusks haven't grown out, but generally steers clear of the adults. Sheltering Seela with their bodies, her mother and aunt swim off.

The polar bear's powerful muscles allow the bear to jump between ice floes or over ice pressure ridges more than 6 feet (2 m) high.
OPPOSITE: *By their first month, walrus calves are strong swimmers. A walrus nurses her calf in the water and, less often, on land or ice.*

Chapter Four

THE HUNT

ringed seals live beneath the Arctic ice, coming up for air every 5 to 15 minutes. They must constantly chew and scrape away at the ice that forms over their breathing holes. The ice is a threat, as it is always about to close off their access to the surface, but it is also an ally, providing seals with protection from predators. Female ringed seals give birth in caves that they dig in the snowdrifts above their breathing holes. In this lair, they keep their pups stashed away while they go out foraging nearby. Often they maintain two or more lairs in their home range, a few miles apart. Concealed in these lairs, they nurse their pups, rest, and hide from polar bears.

Up on the surface of the ice, the cubs' mother listens for sounds coming from below. Nanu and her brother trail behind, watching and keeping quiet.

Under the ice, a ringed seal looks for one of her breathing holes. She rises cautiously, wary that a bear might be staking out the hole. But only a gull is at the surface. After coming up for air, she dives back down into her lair. Nanu's mother catches the seal's scent. She can sniff out a seal through 3 feet (1 m) of snow. She slinks up to the lair. Lifting up her body, she comes smashing down on the ice with her front paws.

The hard ice of the cave's roof doesn't break. She lifts herself back up, crashes down again. The seal, alerted by the thumps, darts into the sea. Ringed seals are nimble. Nineteen times out of twenty, they escape.

A small iceberg, stranded on the shore of Ellesmere Island, Canada, after an ebb tide.

A ringed seal pup lies exposed on the ice. Ringed seals are the smallest and most numerous seals in the Arctic. Their high blubber content makes them a polar bear's favorite prey. OPPOSITE: *Beneath the Arctic ice, a ringed seal rises toward one of her breathing holes, one of several she maintains throughout her home range. Her snow cave can often have several chambers in which she can rest and hide from polar bears.*

Scavenging a polar bear kill, a gull pecks at some scraps. Ravens also eat from bear kills. OPPOSITE: *A polar bear lies in wait at a breathing hole. Although this hunting method takes longer, bears catch more seals and expend less energy by still-hunting than by crashing the ice or charging at the seals.*

Hungry and determined, the cubs' mother walks on, stalking more seals. Ringed seals have good hearing, so she approaches their lairs slowly to make as little noise as possible. She can smell a seal in a breathing hole from more than half a mile away. To learn to hunt, the cubs have to become observant. And they have to follow their mother's example. When they misbehave or don't pay attention, she nips them on the ear, cuffs them softly with her paw, or growls at them.

A seal comes up for air. The bear pounces, jamming herself into the seal's breathing hole. She pulls the seal's body out of the hole with her teeth, then drags it on the ice several yards from the hole. The fox waits patiently, but his bright eyes and the swish of his tail in the snow give away his eagerness to share in the meal.

Nanu and her brother crowd around their mother as she feeds. She bites off the skin and blubber, the only parts of her prey she usually eats. Her body digests fat very efficiently, and seal blubber is rich in calories. Her first meal in six months provides her with enough food to sustain her and let her nurse her cubs. The scavengers gather for the leftovers.

Besides crashing a lair, the bear has another method to trap a seal. Remaining completely still, she lies in wait at a breathing hole, sometimes for hours, until a seal comes up for air. She uses this hunting technique throughout the year. In the summer, she can also ambush seals as they haul out to molt and bask in the sun next to a breathing hole. She creeps up on the ice, breaking into a run as she nears her prey. While charging at a seal, she can run as fast as 25 miles an hour (40 km/h). She can also swim under the ice until she reaches a seal's breathing hole, bursting out of it to grab the seal.

Wandering on the vast ice plain, a polar bear sniffs the air for prey. Bears make seasonal migrations of up to 2,500 miles (4,000 km).

Gregarious by nature, walruses rarely haul out alone. Even when they have space to sprawl out, they prefer to lie next to each other. OPPOSITE: *Each month a calf grows by 4 to 6 inches (10 to 15 cm). Walrus milk is about 30 percent fat, ensuring that a calf will grow quickly.*

Out at sea, all the walruses are riding on a large ice floe. Lying packed together helps them keep warm. And it also lets them warn each other of danger quickly. Seela and her mother have joined the herd. For her safety, her mother had kept her apart from the other walruses. A newborn walrus can get trampled in the shoving, squabbling crowd. Although walruses are extremely sociable and watch out for one another, fighting off attacks to the herd, they habitually quarrel over haul-out spots. Much of this sparring is just for show, stopping as soon as one of the two competitors displays larger tusks. But some walruses continue to wrangle, pushing and climbing over the others until they find a good stretch of ice. Then the bluster ends, and they settle in to loaf or sleep companionably, surrounded by a walrus on every side.

Unlike polar bears, walruses seldom hunt alone. As a herd, they go out in search of their favorite food—clams. They dive down to the seafloor, where the clams lie buried. Clams dig themselves into the mud with their foot and extend their siphon into the water, which allows them to eat, breathe, and filter water.

Using their whiskers like fingers, the walruses feel around the ocean floor for the clams. The walruses squirt jets of water to root out the burrowed clams. Cupping their mouths over their prey, they quickly suck up the soft tissue inside the shells using the pumping action of their thick tongues. After they eat, they leave the empty clamshells behind.

Benthic, or bottom, feeders, walruses eat mollusks, as well as crabs, shrimp, and other invertebrates. A few rogue males feed on seal carrion and young seals.

A walrus can stay underwater for as long as 12 minutes, typically diving to depths of about 30 to 160 feet (10 to 50 m).

Reacting to the disturbance of their clam bed, some of the clams rebury themselves, and some scuttle off. They propel themselves with their foot across the ocean floor. A few neighboring scallops flee, too. Quickly opening and closing their shells, the scallops soar through the water.

A walrus can eat 4,000 or more clams a day. The herd rifles through much of the clam bed. Nevertheless, a few of the clams escape, enough to repopulate the bed eventually. Seela is still too young to hunt or eat clams, but her mother has replenished her milk supply and can nurse her again. The herd, full and drowsy, goes up on the ice floe to sleep.

Seela's herd hunts clams and other shellfish year-round. In summer, the retreat of the ice gives the walruses greater access to food. In the ancient rhythms of the North, though, the days of abundance for Nanu and her family end with the approach of summer and the melting of the ice.

Chapter Five

SUMMER VISITORS

a s summer nears, the days lengthen. Soon, day and night will merge, and the Ice Kingdom will bathe in 24 hours of sun. In the summer, the sun does not set in the Arctic. The heat begins to melt the ice cover, creating leads—breaks in the ice. The sun's rays reach into the leads, sparking an explosion of life.

In the Arctic, species are interconnected, and all are bound by the seasonal freezing and thawing of the ice. Algae and other tiny plants called phytoplankton drift in the ocean and grow at the bottom of the sea ice. As the light of the sun penetrates into the ocean, it sets off photosynthesis. The plants flourish and become food for small crustaceans, such as shrimplike copepods, mysids, and krill. Arctic cod forage under the ice for these zooplankton. Found farther north than any other fish, the cod have antifreeze proteins in their blood that allow them to live in the icy waters. The zooplankton sustain the cod. Ringed seals eat the cod, their main source of food. In turn, the seals feed the polar bears, the species at the top of the Arctic's food chain.

As more of the ice clears, the swarms of plankton and fish soon draw even more predators. Warmer temperatures cause the ice to shift and break up. The ice sheet splits. A crack runs down its thick white mantle for miles. The rift provides a wide sea-lane that flows out to the open ocean. The annual pilgrimage of summer begins.

An iceberg near Baffin Island, Nunavut, Canada.

*During the summer, temperatures in the high Arctic can reach 50 degrees (10°C). As the heat increases,
polar bears become lethargic to keep from overheating.*

Blue-phase arctic foxes, commonly found in the Pribilof and Aleutian Islands of Alaska, molt in summer, but remain darker throughout the year than white-phase foxes.

Born weighing a ton, bowhead whales reach a maximum weight of 200,000 pounds (90,000 kg). The large head of an adult bowhead takes up a third of the whale's body length.

A bowhead whale's wide, triangular fluke arcs up out of the water, then disappears. The enormous bowhead dives for copepods and krill. Behind the whale, a pod of belugas scours under the ice for cod. Belugas and bowheads often travel together. The females of both species will soon have calves. Seabirds also migrate north to give birth. Flying to their nesting cliffs, thick-billed murres stop to feed on cod, squid, and krill, plunging to depths of 600 feet (180 m). Harp seals join the frenzy. They glide and prance along the lead. They are after cod, too. All rush to take part in the banquet. The ice typically clears for only six weeks or so. Then the brief Arctic summer will come to an end, and the ice will once again close over the waters.

Leaping through the air in the open water, some breaching orcas head north as well. Ferocious predators, killer whales eat a range of prey, from herring to whales.

The walrus herds build up their fat reserves for the winter, feasting on the newly available supplies of food. Summer is a time of plenty in the Arctic—for all but the polar bears. Nanu's mother and the other bears had a good hunting season, but now must live mainly on their body fat until the ice returns and they can start hunting the seals again.

Cubs have too little blubber to be in the water for a long time. Nanu and her brother therefore need to stay close to land or ice. So, as the ice retreats, the cubs and their mother must return to the shore.

A harp seal can forage at greater depths than a ringed seal, sometimes diving deeper than 800 feet (240 m).

Known as the canaries of the sea, beluga whales are highly vocal, producing chirps, whistles, clicks, squeals, and other sounds. FOLLOWING PAGES: *Caribou at their herd's spring calving grounds near the Beaufort Sea, Alaska.*

A colony of common murres gathers on a rock. Common murres and thick-billed murres belong to the auk family. Though the two species are similar, common murres have longer, more slender bills than thick-billed murres and usually stay in ice-free waters. OPPOSITE: *A blue-phase arctic fox stalks a thick-billed murre on St. George Island in the Pribilof archipelago of Alaska.*

Adult females without cubs, as well as adult males and subadult bears, are able to continue hunting. They pursue the seals migrating north. A layer of fat more than 4 inches (10 cm) thick keeps them warm as they swim and provides them with buoyancy in the water. But as more of the ice melts away, they have no surface from which to catch the seals, and they, too, must come ashore. On land, the bears feed as they can, eating kelp, scrounging for berries, catching ducks and other birds. While they fast, they sleep and cool off, sprawled out on the ground or lying in pits they dig in the earth. Their fur has molted, becoming thinner to keep them comfortable.

The arctic foxes have also shed their thick winter fur. The darker color of their summer coats provides them with camouflage as they scurry along the coastal cliffs, preying on the murres and their eggs and chicks.

The foxes make their dens in the cliffs near the murres and other seabirds. After raiding the birds, they take their prey to their dens to feed their young. Mating for life, both the male and female foxes care for their kits. The baby foxes, born in spring, mature over the summer. When the foxes have surplus food, they hide it in their dens or among some rocks, where they can retrieve it later.

As summer comes to an end, the arrival of colder weather brings the promise of food again for the polar bears—once the ice returns.

During especially warm summers, walruses haul out on land to rest after feeding in nearby waters. But they prefer to be on the ice, where they are less vulnerable to attack by predators. OPPOSITE: *The young male bears' mock combat prepares them for the more serious brawls they will endure later, when they will compete for a mate.*

Chapter Six

WAITING FOR THE ICE

a s autumn returns, ice forms along the coast, slowly spreading seaward. The Arctic's summer guests migrate back to warmer waters. Its permanent residents prepare for winter. The walruses and the ringed seals travel inshore, closer to the coastline. The polar bears' fur becomes thicker and denser to protect them from the cold. Growing out, the fur of the white-phase foxes once again turns white to blend in with the snow.

Ready to break their summer fast, Nanu and her family wait for their hunting grounds to reform out on the frozen ocean. As the land-fast ice—the ice fastening to the shore—grows, the cubs' mother demonstrates again how to crash the ice, helping them practice for the seal hunts to come. Nanu pays attention. Her brother, less focused, flops head down into the water after breaking through the ice.

For the cubs to survive on their own, they must learn how to hunt, how to protect their kills from being taken from them, and how to recognize danger. Already they know to be wary of adult males. By sparring with her cubs, she makes them more aggressive. This develops their ability to fight and defend themselves. Nipping and advancing on Nanu, she drives Nanu back until Nanu pushes back, swiping at her mother with her paw.

An icy fjord near Pond Inlet at the northeastern end of Baffin Island, Nunavut, Canada.

Polar bear milk is about 30 percent fat. To produce the rich milk, a polar bear mother must catch enough food to sustain both herself and her young.
OPPOSITE: *A polar bear walks across the pack ice. In summer and fall, bears hunt for ringed seals and other prey at the edge of the pack ice.*

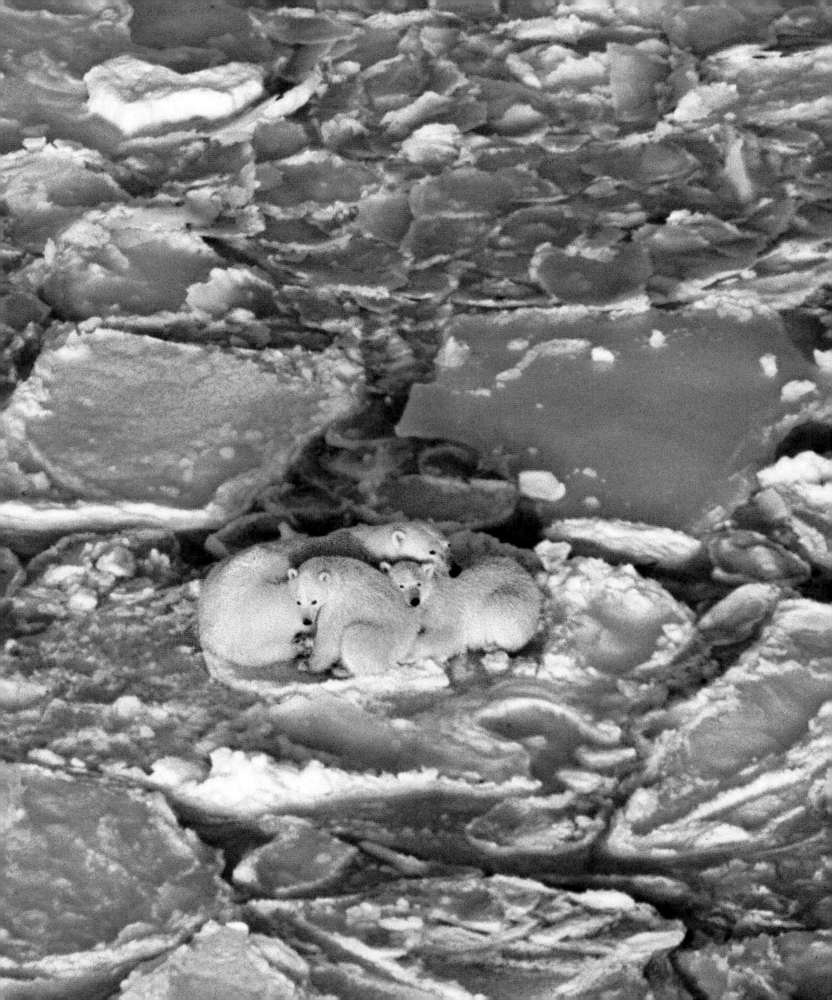

Hunting for prey in the melting ice, a bear walks between ice floes. A bear's average walking speed is 3.4 miles an hour (5.5 km/h). OPPOSITE: *A polar bear mother and her cubs rest on some cracked and broken sea ice in Wapusk National Park, Manitoba, Canada.*

Each day grows darker. The long polar night returns. The ice now reaches for miles out to sea. Nanu's mother leads her cubs out across the wide ice field to resume hunting. But the ice is different this year. It is thin and elastic, and rolls as they walk on it. Nanu yelps and sits down, not sure of her footing. Her mother walks gingerly across the ice. In some spots, it hasn't hardened enough yet to support her weight. Farther ahead, the ice is still broken up. She turns and chuffs at them. Her call signals that they have to go back. She returns with them to the ice nearer the shore, ice they can trust. Until more of the ocean freezes, they will remain hungry.

The amount of ice cover has always varied somewhat from year to year, depending on the weather. In the past, the ice usually formed in autumn and remained through June. Now, the ice is melting earlier in the spring and freezing later in the fall. Over the last 20 years, the ice in the Arctic has shrunk by 4 to 8 percent per decade. And temperatures in the sea and the air have grown warmer, causing changes that are testing the animals' ancient ways of survival.

Huddled together, Nanu and her family wait for the ice to become solid. Seela's herd looks for ice strong enough to hold them. Scattered over miles and isolated from each other, the walruses haul out wherever they can find a stretch of ice. Finally,

With open water all around, a walrus rests alone on an ice floe. As sea temperatures rise, ice in Arctic

A harp seal mother watches her pup from her breathing hole. Female harp seals give birth on the pack ice, nursing their pups for 12 days. OPPOSITE: *Harp seal pups cannot swim for their first few weeks of life. Recently, the melting pack ice has caused thousands of pups to drown in eastern Canada.*

The cubs and their mother spend the winter roaming on their hunting grounds. More independent now, the cubs crowd her less than they used to. They eat from her kills but continue to nurse, still depending on her milk for survival. Spring comes again—and that means a new supply of seal pups. She continues to teach them how to find the pups' birth lairs and pound through the ice to catch the hidden seals. This year, however, more of the pups seem to be exposed on the ice. Rising temperatures have either melted their lairs or thinned the ice cover so much that their mothers didn't have enough snow and ice to dig a cave. Without the shelter of the ice, the pups risk being eaten by predators or dying from the cold.

Nanu's mother sees a pup lying next to a breathing hole. The pup's mother raises her head out of the hole to check on her pup. All seems well. Her head disappears back down the hole. Nanu's mother skulks toward the pup, then charges. But the pup slips into the hole in time. Looking for another chance to hunt, she notices some gulls flying toward a spot farther away on the ice. A meal must be nearby. She heads in the birds' direction to find out what they are scavenging. The cubs follow her as she swims near the ice edge. The kill is just yards away. Asleep near it, though, lies a large male bear.

Hunger forces her to take an unusual risk. Weighing half a ton, the male bear is twice as big as she is. She leads her cubs past the bear to feed on the leftovers. They steal a few bites. Nanu turns to look at the bear, her mother's training and her own instincts making her alert. Maybe they can fill up before he wakes up. The bear sees them. Growling and snarling, he scares them off. They lope away. Although they have escaped, they are still hungry and must once again go on the hunt for food.

An adult bear can consume up to 150 pounds (68 kg) of blubber during a feeding. The fat provides the bear with both energy and water.
OPPOSITE: *A bear naps after a meal. As bears eat, they bite off large chunks of blubber, swallowing them without chewing.*

Chapter Seven

WINTER STORM

e very winter, the animals of the North must withstand fierce storms. Temperatures can drop below minus 40 degrees (-40°C) during a blizzard. But the increasing temperatures in the Arctic have created a new threat for the inhabitants of the Ice Kingdom. When the temperatures were colder year-round, solid ice once shielded the coast. Without this protection, storm winds slam harder into the shore. As more of the sea ice melts, the level of the sea has also increased, leading to higher waves and coastal erosion as the waves pound the shore. So while the weather is warmer, winter conditions along the shoreline have paradoxically grown even harsher than before.

A heavy storm heralds the onset of winter. Along the coast, snow billows off the cliffs and ripples across the ice at the shore. A male bear plods through the squall. An arctic fox hurries across the ice plain, trying to resist the buffeting of the wind. Seela's herd heads into deeper waters to ride out the storm.

Out at sea, ice floes have not formed yet. The walruses endure the battering of the wind and the ocean without a chance to haul out and rest. The herd struggles to stay together. A strong current separates Seela from her mother. Seela loses sight of the herd. Barking, she cries for help. Her mother and aunt search desperately for her but can't find her. And now the high, rolling waves sweep her farther and farther from her mother and the herd.

A lone polar bear on the ice cap of Northeast Land, Northeast Svalbard Nature Reservation, Norway.

A polar bear sniffs for prey in near whiteout conditions. The coldest temperature recorded in the Arctic was -90°F (-67.8°C) at the village of Verkhoyansk, Siberia.

As an adult, this baby walrus will have a massive skull capable of bashing through more than 8 inches (20 cm) of ice.

Increasingly warm winters are causing polar bears in some areas of the Arctic to shift their diet from ringed seals to harbor seals and bearded seals, which depend less on the ice. OPPOSITE: *In the past 50 years, average winter temperatures in Alaska and western Canada have risen as much as 7 degrees (4°C).* FOLLOWING PAGES: *Evening light in a glaciated valley of Baffin Island, Canada.*

On land, the storm builds in intensity. The wind reaches 80 miles an hour (129 km/h). The cubs and their mother walk through the blizzard, looking for food. Little is visible in the whiteout.

Nanu turns around. Her brother is far behind. All three are starving, but he is tiring faster than his mother and sister. His legs buckle. He lies down on the snow. His mother calls to him, a plea for him to get up. Obeying, he lifts himself and walks a few steps. He sinks down again. Nanu and her mother snuggle up next to him to keep him warm.

The snow streams down on them. He has always been a little more fragile than his sister, and he grows weaker day by day. The storm lets up slightly. His mother probes and sniffs around him, checking his condition. Maybe he can regain his strength. But he is too hungry and exhausted to continue. Snow covers him, piling in drifts over his body.

His mother and sister stay at his side. Nanu licks her mother's face. Cold air blows sheets of snow up on the ridges of ice around them. They have to leave. As they stride across the ice, their fur undulates from the wind. They turn around for one last look. A searching glance, as if they want one final confirmation that he will not be coming with them. They forge on. They have to keep walking until they find food, or they, too, will die.

A mother and calf in Foxe Basin, home of the largest walrus herd in Canada. Depleted after centuries of hunting, Atlantic walruses are far less numerous than Pacific walruses. OPPOSITE: *Most walruses have 18 teeth, including their tusks. They use their sensitive whiskers to identify each other, explore the ocean floor for shellfish, and grasp food.*

In the sea, Seela clings to life. Bobbing on the surface of the water, she floats to conserve her energy, her flippers folded on her chest, her head above the water. But she can't last much longer. The herd searches for her. Her mother and aunt refuse to give up. Following a strong current, they travel farther out to sea, and it leads them right to Seela.

Her mother clasps her with her flippers. Comforted but still weary, Seela climbs on her mother's back for a ride. A walrus mother's bond to her calf is one of the strongest maternal attachments among all mammals. Whenever Seela gets tired, her mother gives her a ride to let her rest out of the water.

Seela's rescue is a small miracle, a testament to how deeply walruses cherish their young. A walrus population regenerates slowly, and it takes years for a walrus to become an adult. Each calf is therefore vital to the herd. Walrus mothers give birth to a single calf during each pregnancy, devoting themselves to their calf for more than two years. Female walruses, known as cows, mature earlier than the males. The bulls do not reach their full growth until they are more than a decade old, when they become large and strong enough to fight other males for a mate.

Winter draws to a close. Seela now has small tusks. Having sprouted during her first summer, they will continue to grow, eventually reaching a couple of feet in length. Click, knock, clang. Seela hears strange sounds. The odd music comes from a group of males nearby. Using the large pouches around their necks, they are making the bell-like tones to attract a mate. Stationed about 30 feet (9 m) apart, the males sing, competing to lure a female through their serenade. A male can sing for hours on end, sometimes for more than 50 hours straight.

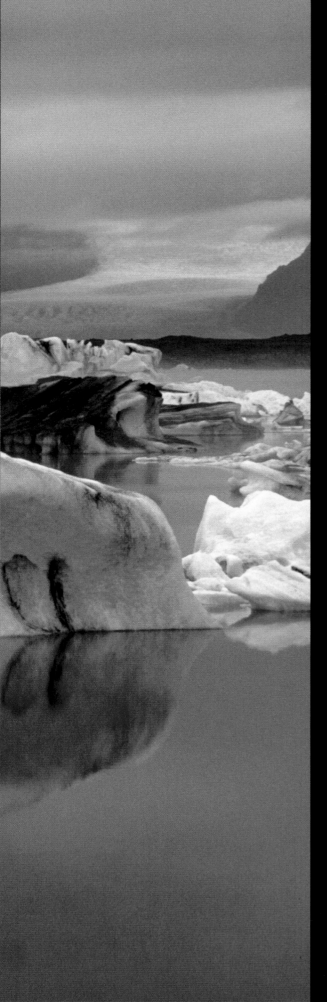

Chapter Eight

ON HER OWN

t wo years old now, Seela and Nanu take different paths, representative of their species. While Seela stays with her herd, continuing to live with the protection of a community, Nanu must become independent and fend for herself. Polar bears are solitary predators. Her mother grows distant. And, one morning, growling and walking threateningly toward her, she drives her away. A bear's home range can extend for more than a hundred thousand square miles. They may never see each other again.

Still an adolescent, Nanu is vulnerable but must now embark on a life alone. Her mother has taught her how to hunt and how to groom herself. When her fur is clean, it provides her with better insulation. By watching her mother, she has also learned how to dig a temporary snow den where she can hide on the coldest days. She has learned the basic skills she needs to subsist in the Arctic. Like all polar bears, however, she has to adapt to new situations, calling on her instinctive resourcefulness to find food and protect herself from danger.

The next few years will be the most challenging of Nanu's life. Not yet an experienced hunter, she risks losing her kills to older and stronger adults. Her mother prepared her for life on the ice. But the changing conditions in her homeland will force her to adopt new strategies in order to survive. Again this spring, warm weather arrives earlier than in the past. The ice field floods. Without a surface to hunt the seals, Nanu has no choice but to head out from the coast, traveling to ice beyond the range she knows.

Icebergs calved from the Icelandic glacier of Vatnajökull.

A polar bear in Churchill, Manitoba, plays with a snowball. Each fall, bears congregate along the coastline near the town while waiting for the ice to return. OPPOSITE: *A mother bear shoos off her young when the cubs are ready to be on their own and she is ready to mate again. Cubs may be forced out on their own early if their mother dies or becomes too lean to nurse.*

Like walrus tusks, a narwhal's tusk is a canine tooth. Growing out of a male narwhal's upper left jaw, it pokes through the whale's lip and reaches up to 9 feet (2.7 m) in length. OPPOSITE: *An arctic fox yowls to court a mate. The fox's bark carries over a wide distance. The fox mating season occurs in spring.*

As she walks on the ice, a flock of thick-billed murres lands in water nearby. Splash, she leaps into the sea after them. The birds will only be a mouthful apiece. But hungry, she will eat anything, and they are well worth trying for. She has no chance of catching them. Diving farther than she can, they fly through the ocean, beating their black wings as though they were up in the sky.

The murres disappear into the depths. Nanu can stay underwater for only two minutes. Turning around in the water to go up for air, she sees an even stranger sight: creatures with a long, spiral tusk. Back on the surface, her paws resting on the ice, she takes another look. A tusk rises out of a break in the ice, then another, and two more. Nanu has come upon a herd of narwhals—the unicorns of the sea.

Following close behind one another, the narwhals come up for air in the tight space of the lead. The bounty of the local waters is now open to them. Best of all, they have a passageway to a new hoard of their favorite fish, arctic cod.

A narwhal's ivory tusk has 10 million nerve endings. Extremely sensitive, it may help the whales detect slight shifts in pressure, temperature, salt level, and other factors in the water and air. Rarely studied and hard to track, much of their behavior remains a mystery. But however they sense their surroundings, they seem to know when the ice is about to break up. The narwhals find small gaps in the ice as they swim north to feed and have their young.

The ice cover shrinks rapidly, breaking up sooner and more abruptly than before. Nanu has to pick her way through jagged ice. A fox has been following her, but has to turn back as she paddles out into an open stretch of water. Arctic foxes can't swim for long distances. Without her, the fox will have to find another source of food. Nanu faces her own predicament. Stranded on shattered ice, she has never been so hungry.

An opportunistic feeder, a polar bear hunts many types of seals, as well as seabirds and occasionally much larger prey, such as beluga whales.

Leaping, a polar bear jumps between ice floes. Ice in the Arctic has been breaking up sooner and freezing later than usual, challenging the bears' ability to hunt. OPPOSITE: *A polar bear emerges from a swim. Bears wash with water or slide on the snow to clean themselves after every meal.*

ISLAND REFUGE

Out on the water, Seela's herd has scattered to haul out on the few ice floes left in the warmer summer ocean. The cramped space sets off bickering. Roaring, the walruses battle for the choicest spots. Some thrust their tusks at each other. One swats another with a flipper. Several raise their tusks, showing them off to get the other walruses to back down. Walruses display their tusks to bully one another. In walrus society, the longer the tusks, the higher the rank.

Seela has never been through a bad ice year. The adults have, though never one this severe. Finally, one walrus triggers a collective decision to abandon the shrinking ice. The walrus dives in the water. The rest then plunge in, too. They will have to search for a new home—on land—to use as a platform on which to rest between foraging hunts. Although walruses haul out on coastal or island beaches when the summers are particularly warm, they prefer to stay on the ice, where they have better access to feeding grounds. On land, they are more awkward, and could be more vulnerable to attack. But the lack of ice has left Seela's herd no choice but to leave.

The walruses can't go to the shore, as polar bear mothers are on the coast with their cubs, so they head to sea to find a distant island where they can be safe. In the open water, the herd will face many perils: fatigue, cold, separation, and—the most dangerous threat of all—killer whales. Polar bears and humans are the walruses' only other predators.

In late June, a fogbow appears on the horizon in Igloolik, Nunavut, Canada.

Walruses crowd together on one of the last remaining ice floes as the warmer weather melts the ice. Soon it will no longer hold all of their weight.

Two bull walruses spar over a haul-out spot. During the walrus mating season, the males also fight to keep other males out of their breeding sites.

Nanu is standing on a raft of ice. Should she stay on the remnants of ice, where she can't find food, or follow the scent of the migrating prey out into the unknown sea?

Now is the time to be bold—but not hasty. Tentatively, she backs into the water. She is reluctant to leave the ice floe. But to survive, she must now risk everything and go beyond what her mother has taught her.

Despite the warmer temperatures, the ocean remains cold, staying only a few degrees above freezing. Nanu has put on enough fat to let her swim for up to 60 miles (96 km) at a stretch. Her layer of blubber and her oily fur coat, which repels water, protect her as she swims. Alone in the ocean, with nothing but water all around, she has to keep swimming until she finds ice or land.

Paddling with his front paws, a polar bear uses his back paws to steer. Two layers of fur provide insulation in the frigid water.

Thick-billed murres raise their chicks in the cliffs. When the birds are ready to travel south to their wintering grounds, their chicks, only three weeks old and still unable to fly, must hurl themselves from the cliffs into the ocean. They are joined in the water by their fathers to begin a long migration at sea.

The walruses swim day and night for a week until they finally reach an island. At last, landfall. Exhausted by traveling without a chance to haul out, they now face the last and most difficult stretch of the trip. They survey the hard, rocky slope.

Braving the climb, they inch up the shore, hoisting themselves with their flippers. Some of the males weigh more than a ton. Several of the walruses slide back into the water. They try again, lifting themselves up the slippery bank. Seela makes it up the rocks. Safe on land, worn out, the herd drops off to sleep.

Arriving here first, a male bear has already staked out the walruses. Hungry but patient, he hides out of sight, waiting for the best opportunity to strike.

Thousands of thick-billed murres have come to this small offshore island to breed. The noisy birds fly around the cliffs and land on the narrow ledges, where they raise their chicks. A fox prowls near the birds. Although the island is far out at sea, the fox became stranded here when the pack ice retreated. Looking for food in winter, arctic foxes can cover hundreds of miles. The fox, already in summer camouflage, doesn't need to scavenge from the bear. The large murre colony provides the fox with a feast of chicks.

To avoid gulls, foxes, and other predators, thick-billed murres don't build nests. Female murres lay a single egg on the rock of a steep cliff face. Pointed at one end, murre eggs roll in a circle if they are disturbed, keeping them from falling off the high ledges, where they are incubated for about a month.

Both parents sit on the egg, taking turns feeding in the sea. After the egg hatches, they continue to alternate care. One parent broods the chick, while the other dives into the ocean to feed and bring fish back to the chick.

Walruses sometimes find places to rest near the water in case they need to escape a predator. Here, one walrus displays his tusks to establish dominance among the herd. OPPOSITE: *Shielded from attack by the bodies of the older walruses, the calves lie toward the center of the herd.* FOLLOWING PAGES: *Calm waters near the island of Spitsbergen, Norway.*

The walruses sprawl on the rocks, resting and sunning themselves. Temperatures climb well above freezing. Their skin starts to flush. It turns pink, shading into a bright, rusty red the longer they are out in the sun. The increased blood flow in their fat outer layer helps them cool off. The capillaries on their skin dilate, which allows some of their body heat to dissipate. The walruses begin to molt, gradually shedding their old hair and skin.

Molting causes their skin to itch. To get rid of the itch, they scratch every which way. They rub with their front flippers. They scrape with their back flippers. One walrus twists against the rocks, using the rough surface as a back scratcher.

Seela goes up on the bluffs, wandering away from the herd. Her aunt starts to follow her as she climbs higher and higher. Seela disappears from sight. Her aunt calls out. No response. Seela's brief adventure on her own has taken a terrifying turn. Now trapped on a thin ledge, she must either jump through a narrow opening in the sharp rocks below or risk being eaten by the bear just a few feet away.

Straddling two cliffs, the bear carefully makes his way toward her. Seela throws herself into the sea. She lands safely. Then, racing to the herd, she swims back toward the rocks where the walruses are resting and barks, alerting them to the danger. Frantic, the walruses topple into the sea, sliding, rolling, crashing into each other.

Seela reunites with her mother and aunt. They flee with the herd to a rocky beach on another part of the island. Many other herds have gathered near the beach, all driven here by the disappearance of the ice. At the shore, the male bear bides his time. Stalking the walruses, he tracks their scent and follows them to their new hauling grounds.

A bear searches for prey as he walks through the tundra. Bears are thought to be most active during the early part of the day. OPPOSITE: *To preserve his energy in the summer warmth, a bear rests on the rocks.*

In the sea, Nanu is approaching the island. Catching a ride on an isolated ice floe saved her life, allowing her to rest and regain her strength. But she has been swimming for hours and needs to rest again and eat. Following the scent of the herd, she comes ashore. She sees the huge brown throng of walruses, all crowded together along the beach.

Starving, she acts impulsively. She tries a direct assault, walking straight up to them. The adults are too big for her to take on, but she might be able to pick off a young or injured walrus. The walruses lumber into the sea. A less experienced hunter than the male bear, Nanu doesn't scare them as much. They move to get away from her, but her presence does not cause them to panic.

The walruses haul out on another rocky jetty. Nanu watches them from a distance. For a moment, she and Seela glimpse one another—once separated by a wide distance at birth, they are now both far from home, forced together by the changes in the ice.

One after another, the walruses fall asleep. The male bear sneaks up from the sea. Walruses have a good sense of smell, but he swims up to them from downwind. The walruses wake up to find him almost among them, climbing up the rock where they are resting. Some bolt into the water. Others attack him, wielding their tusks. Undeterred, he pushes forward. He grabs Seela.

Her aunt, already at the water's edge, turns around and climbs back up the slippery rock. She stabs him with her tusks. As he turns to fight her off, Seela escapes into the sea.

A herd flees into the water as a bear approaches. Although walruses are much larger than polar bears, the bears will attack if given the opportunity, and remain a threat. OPPOSITE: *In the water, walruses use their back flippers to propel themselves and their front flippers to steer.*

The bear leaps on Seela's aunt. Seela waits in the water, but her aunt does not return. Her aunt has given her life to protect her. Walruses shield their calves from attack, preserving the species. Her aunt's act has saved Seela's life.

Nanu has to rely on herself to survive. Without food, she will not last much longer. She knows the male will defend his kill. And that he could be dangerous. So she will have to call on her aggressive instincts and be bold. Nanu approaches the bear to share some of his kill. She walks slowly toward him, keeping her head down. Polar bears allow other bears to eat from their kill if the bears assume a submissive position. She is observing proper bear protocol. But it fails to sway him. He runs her off. She tries again. He snarls and chases her away. On her third try, she holds firm. Refusing to give in, she stays put, remaining standing, head lowered, until he accepts to let her eat.

Chapter Ten

HOME AGAIN

for the next four years, Nanu and Seela swim back to the island, driven to return to this rocky outpost by the thinning of the ice. Each year, their stay draws longer. The steadily increasing temperatures have made a demanding world even more difficult, disrupting the ancient rhythm of the seasons, gradually dissolving the Ice Kingdom, turning animals long adapted to the snow and ice into refugees. Walruses feed only in the ocean and find new locations to hunt by riding on the ice. Polar bears are as comfortable on land as on the ice. But using the ice they can catch more prey, and marine mammals are richer in fat than the food the bears can hunt on land.

As the bears' summer fast lengthens, they are losing more weight, affecting their ability to live and reproduce. Scientists predict a 30 percent decline in polar bear populations over the next 45 years. And walruses are also growing more vulnerable. The prolonged melting of the ice may limit their access to food, reducing their numbers and forcing walrus mothers to abandon their calves.

Holed up on the island, Nanu and Seela's herd must wait for the ice to return, watching for signs of its arrival. The temperature drops. Snow builds up on the cliffs. A larger, older walrus makes a decision that the rest of the herd follows. The sea ice—home—beckons. He dives into the sea and the others plunge in behind. Nanu, as eager to return to her hunting ground, also makes her way back to the coastal sea, swimming and leaping onto ice floes.

Peaks in the high Arctic mountain range of the Niels Holgersen Nunatakker, East Greenland.

A bear walks through icy willow shrubs near Hudson Bay. The western shore of the bay has the world's highest concentration of polar bears.
OPPOSITE: *By standing on its hind legs, a curious bear can see farther and detect more odors. Males may track the scent of a breeding female for more than 60 miles (100 km).*

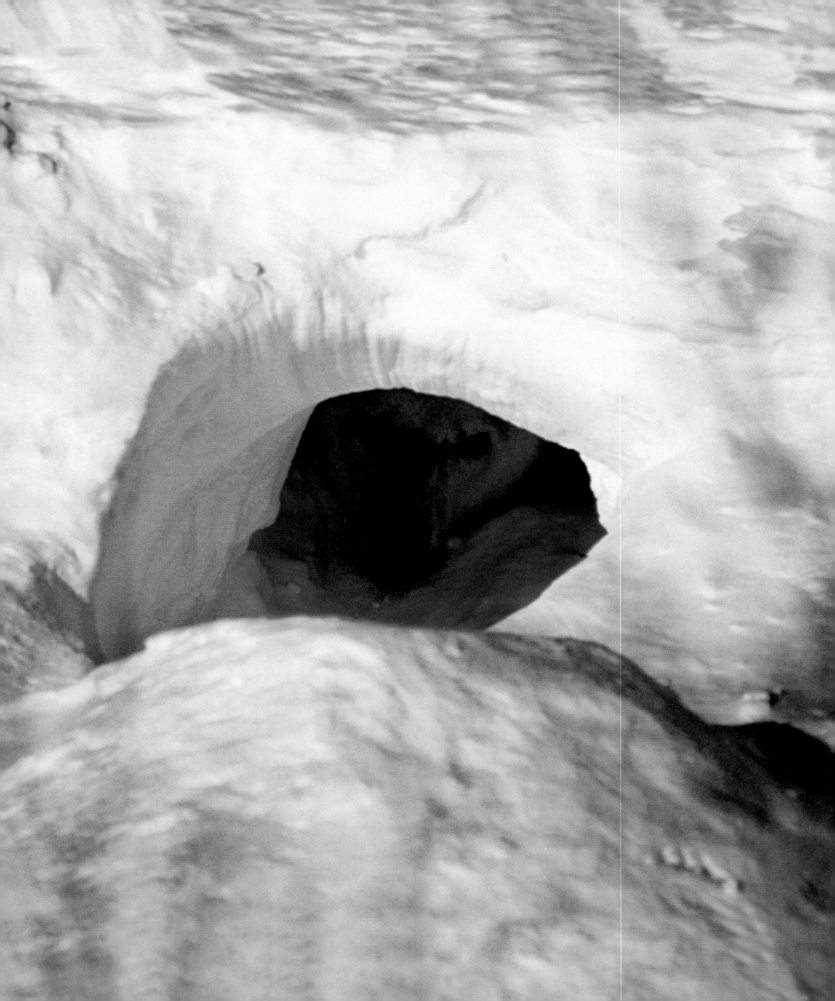

The polar bear mating season peaks in late April and early May. Two males compete for a female. Though often violent, these fights are rarely fatal. OPPOSITE: *A bear looks out from a snow den. Both males and females sometimes build temporary hideouts during fierce weather, but only pregnant females spend months in a den.*

Out on the sea ice, a male bear courts Nanu. Spring has arrived, and the polar bear mating season has begun. Fully grown, she is now ready to mate. He has found her by tracking her scent. Gently biting and wrestling, the two bears become familiar with one another. And so begins an ancient communion that is perhaps of special importance in a disappearing world.

Nanu and her mate spend more than a week together. Mating several times a day induces her to ovulate. Her eggs won't implant until fall, when she will dig her maternity den. This delay ensures that her embryos will not begin to grow until she has built up her fat reserves and has found a safe home in which to give birth to her cubs.

Polar bears are polygynous. The females typically mate with only one male during the breeding season, while the males mate with several females. After Nanu and her mate part, they will probably never see each other again. In three years, when she is ready to mate again, she will have another partner.

Walruses descend from bearlike animals, and share similarities with polar bears. Like the bears, they are polygynous, and a walrus pregnancy includes a delayed implantation. The walrus mating season occurs in winter, but a walrus embryo does not continue to develop until June, when the females begin to stock up during the height of the summer feeding season. This helps to insure that they will have enough of a fat supply to provide for their young.

Heavy from her pregnancy, Nanu slowly makes her way from the shore toward the mountains where she was born. She has put on several hundred pounds of fat. She will live on this stored fat while she is in the maternity den. The fat will also help her produce milk for her cubs. The mountains have less snow than in the past, but she eventually finds a good location and enough snow to start building a den. Shoveling the snow aside with her large paws, she digs an entrance tunnel and a cave several feet wide. Sheltered from the wind, her den faces south to get the best exposure to the sun. Warm and secure in her den, she curls up to sleep.

Months go by. In dens throughout the area, pregnant polar bears are resting before the arrival of their cubs. Outside, in the endless night of winter, the lights of the aurora borealis play against the sky.

In the sea, the male walruses have launched into their yearly rivalry for a mate. Seela and the other females rest on some ice floes. Each male has staked out a breeding site near the females. Performing in their own patch of water, the males vie for the attention of the females through their songs. Learned from listening to other males and taking years of practice to perfect, the mating call of a male walrus is one of the most complex courtship songs among all marine mammals. The males sing underwater, producing a series of bell tones, then loud knocks. Coming up for air, they look around to see if their singing has intrigued a potential mate.

Seela and several other females are watching as they sing. The repetitive taps, knocks, and clanks attract interest. One by one, the walruses pair off. After choosing a male, a female leaves the ice and goes off with the male, mating in the water.

To entice a mate, walrus bulls display their tusks and sing for hours during the walrus mating season. Starting in midwinter, the ritual reaches its peak in February and March.

Like a hand or paw, the front flipper of a walrus has five digits, the vestiges of the walrus's ancestry as a land animal.

The muzzle of a walrus has hundreds of quill-like whiskers called vibrissae.

A walrus female chooses her mate. The males' bell-like tones are produced through the air sacs in their inflatable throat pouches. OPPOSITE: *By July, the sea ice off Admiralty Inlet on the northwest coast of Baffin Island has melted. The island in the province of Nunavut is the largest in Canada.*

Seela is the only one left on the ice. She is not yet ready to succumb to any of her suitors. A persistent male tries to beguile her with his song. Intent on impressing her, he continues singing. Finally, she joins him in the sea. Diving, nuzzling, swooping around one another, they become acquainted. Coming up to the surface, they touch muzzles, identifying one another through the touch of their whiskers.

They remain together briefly. After they separate, he mates with other females, while she begins the long process of becoming a mother. The gestation of a walrus lasts 15 to 16 months.

Chapter Eleven

TWIN CUBS—
AND A CALF

Up in her mountain den, Nanu becomes a mother. Like her mother, she has two cubs. Polar bears usually have twins. She gives birth to a female cub, then a male cub. Their eyes are closed. Blind and helpless, they crawl up her body and start to nurse by instinct. She licks them. This not only cleans them, it helps to stimulate their breathing. To keep them warm, she draws them to her gently with her paw. They stay close to her for their first few weeks, spending most of their time nursing and sleeping.

In the sanctuary of the den, they develop quickly. At about three and a half weeks, they begin to hear. A week later, their eyes open. Their teeth come in. The cubs' fur grows out, allowing them to become more independent. Their fur is now thick enough to protect them from the cold. After they start to walk, they romp around the den, chasing each other. Playing develops their muscles, preparing them for their first trip outside.

By their third month, they are ready to leave the den and follow her out into the spring light. Nanu's cubs emerge from the comfort of their den into a white world of cold and snow, and like other cubs, they are curious but tentative, but soon will begin to explore their new home.

A lacework of ice near the island of Igloolik in Foxe Basin, Nunavut, Canada.

Two cubs peer out while their mother sleeps. Twins make up about 70 percent of all polar bear births. OPPOSITE: *A nursing bear rests to conserve her energy. After months of fasting in her den, a polar bear mother may lose almost half her weight.*

A walrus mother cradles her baby. To protect her calf from danger, a walrus will sometimes clutch her calf with her flippers before diving into the sea. OPPOSITE: *A newborn walrus, just days old. The calf already has a full mustache. As walruses age, their fur becomes less dense and lighter in color.* FOLLOWING PAGES: *Migrating to their calving grounds in spring, caribou travel through the valley of the Kongakut River in Alaska's Arctic National Wildlife Refuge.*

The following spring, Seela becomes a mother, too. She gives birth on an isolated ice floe. Apart from the herd, her calf won't risk being accidentally crushed by other walruses. Seela's calf is 4 feet (1.2 m) long, four times the size of the polar bear cubs.

Seela leads her calf into the water and holds her baby with her front flippers. Head above water, her calf barks and looks around with inquisitive eyes. Their whiskers touch as they nuzzle. A young female walrus joins them. A new trio: a new calf, a new mother, and a new aunt. Standing guard over the newborn, the young female watches for predators, checking in every direction.

In the years ahead, Seela and her helper will devote themselves to protecting the newest member of the herd. Her calf must learn how to swim, haul out, and hunt. And now Seela, like Nanu—and like their mothers before them—sets out to teach her newborn the ways of the ice.

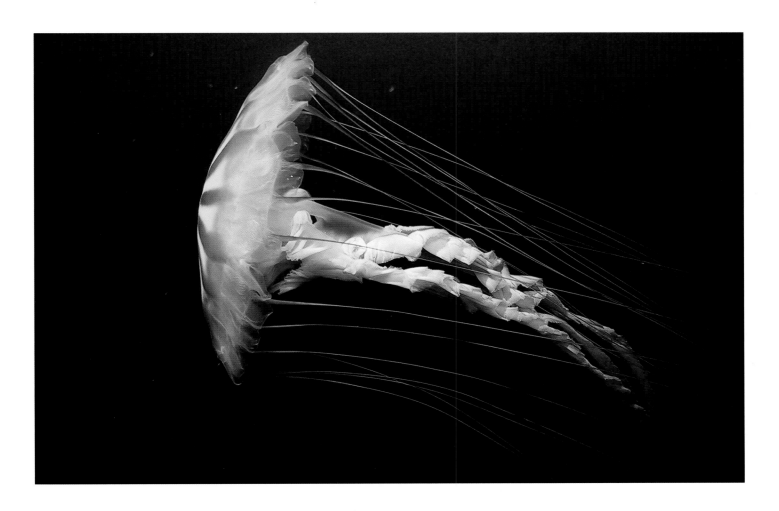

A 10-foot-long (3 m) sea nettle, spotted with the aid of a remotely operated vehicle (ROV) in the deep waters of the Canada Basin. OPPOSITE: *A harp seal pup swims gracefully in the Gulf of St. Lawrence, Canada, one of two breeding sites for harp seals in the western North Atlantic.*

All around the Arctic, the children of the ice make their way into the world as they have for thousands of years. The annual riot of wildlife, which began with the northern migration, now brings forth young. Ducklings paddle behind their mothers. Narwhal and beluga calves swim by their mothers' side. Murre chicks huddle on cliffsides, diligently guarded. Fox kits learn how to hunt. The newborns get their start in life when the weather grows warm enough for them to survive and food becomes more plentiful and easily available for their parents.

Retreating, then returning, and in the past always dependable, the ice preserves the balance of life here. All of the animals' fates are forever tied to the shifting rhythms of the ice that defines their existence, their lives wrapped in the blanket of cold that keeps this kingdom theirs.

What will their children do if it disappears?

What will ours?

Since the 1970s the Arctic's summer sea ice has shrunk by 20 percent. If the current trend continues, the Arctic Ocean could be virtually ice-free in the summer of 2040.

A male king eider in Foxe Basin. The Canadian Arctic is a major nesting area for this duck and other migratory seabirds.

Yawning and molting, an arctic hare sheds his winter fur. His coat turns blue-gray in spring to blend with the tundra.
OPPOSITE: *A glacial lake in the Canadian island of Devon, the largest uninhabited island on Earth.*

Chapter Twelve

THE MAKING OF
ARCTIC TALE

Adam Ravetch & Sarah Robertson

O ur journey began 15 years ago with a monster: the walrus. Local legends reported that the animal could hold a man against his will, knock his head off with its tusks, and, then, suck his brains out. Who knew that one day it would result in a feature film?

We were young photographers at the beginning of our careers, looking for a niche in the world from which we could bring back unusual images. The beauty of the north captivated us, as did the notion that the Arctic was little known, its many secrets hidden under the ice.

Few people had been in the water with the walruses when we first began filming them. The promise of discovering new animal behavior and bringing back images that no one had seen before was a big motivator. The richness of the unknown Arctic was an exciting and challenging prospect for us. But as we gained experience, it was the animals themselves that drew us back year after year.

The walrus and polar bear amazed us. Their capability to learn and their remarkable dedication to their babies really impressed us. We knew that if we could capture these traits on film, we could get people to admire these animals as much as we did. So, we started filming throughout dozens of regions of Canada and other polar countries.

In *Arctic Tale,* Nanu and Seela are composite characters of many of the individual animals that we photographed on our northern journeys. They represent the best of their species; they embody the heart and the spirit intrinsic to so many of the polar bears and walruses we encountered.

Working in the north also drew us close to a lot of highly skilled people. Dozens of Inuit hunters and guides helped us find and live close to the animals. We worked with some of the best polar cinematographers in the world and spent months at a time camping on the land and boating in the sea, searching and waiting, learning and experiencing the Arctic.

We quietly collected more than 800 hours of moving images. We did not take large film crews with assistants and mounds of equipment. We are minimalists. The best images were always obtained with simple machines and with only one or two people.

After traveling across the ice-covered ocean by skidoo and sled, filmmaker Adam Ravetch waits at an open lead, where animals sometimes seek refuge.

There are no masters of the Arctic, and very little luck. If you get something out of the north, it is because people work together, with infinite patience and knowledge, to achieve spectacular results. Many hands put in hundreds of hours of struggle and sacrifice to help us reach our goal.

Most Arctic suffering comes from the psychological rather than the physical. Overcoming the cold is possible; overcoming the obstacles of the mind is far more difficult. Accepting the loneliness of the Arctic was perhaps the hardest thing. There are weeks of isolated silence, staring at an empty landscape, waiting for animals to appear or for weather to clear.

And then, suddenly the Arctic reveals herself without warning. A planned shoot of a week or two rarely would produce anything. It takes months of waiting, anticipating. Then, in an instant, all the elements fall into place, the stars are aligned, and there is a fleeting chance to capture what we have been waiting for—the narwhals appear from nowhere, a polar bear pounces. It's a moment of ecstasy, made special after worrying so long. But the window of opportunity can close as quickly as it comes. If a moment of magic is not seized upon when it appears, the entire season's offerings could be lost.

We can count on our hands these magical days when we achieved many of the greatest moments in *Arctic Tale.*

DIVING WITH WALRUS (TOLD BY ADAM RAVETCH)

In 1990, the walrus seemed like a bizarre animal to us: a ton of blubber, massive tapered tusks, and downright ugly. But to many people of the north, the very mention of its name evoked instant fear. It was a monster and like all monsters, it was connected to some fabulous mythology.

Adam Ravetch films at the rocky island shown in the movie and emerges from a dive under the ice. A day at the office with the team: husband and wife filmmakers Adam Ravetch and Sarah Robertson, cinematographer Rob Garrard, Inuit guide Timuit Qammukaq—and the walruses. OPPOSITE: *Adam dives under the ice canopy, where a bloom of algae has begun to grow. Phytoplankton are the first link in the Arctic food chain. Diminishing sea ice prevents their growth, which may threaten the entire food web.*

I first started hearing the stories from the Inuit hunters. I was thinking about swimming with the walruses, something that had rarely been done, but I was told to be very cautious. The walrus, they said, can sneak behind you and grab you with its massive flippers. It can smash your head off with a smack of its tusks, they warned, and then suck your brains out.

The story sounded far-fetched. Yet, later, I learned some walruses had been seen holding seals between their flippers and sucking the meat right out of their skins. That story, and the fact that walruses are 2,000-pound beasts armed with daggerlike tusks, made me approach the whole project very carefully.

We designed and built a cage for protection underwater. Surprisingly, it worked. The first walruses we tried it on were aggressive, and being inside the cage was terrifying. Over time however, it allowed us to swim next to the walruses and to record some of the first extensive moving images of these animals underwater.

While slow and lumbering out of the water, walruses are graceful and fluid underwater. With a flexible backbone and movable joints, the walrus can change its shape underwater, elongating its body, making it a captivating subject to photograph. The most surprising thing we learned was that walruses are always touching—a flipper resting on a neighbor's, a head nuzzled under a chin, or a whole "rumba" line of walruses seeking comfort from one another.

Nowhere was this more apparent than with walrus mothers, who held on tightly to their calves with their broad flippers. We saw mothers constantly reassuring their 200-pound infants with kisses and nuzzles against their sensitive whiskers. So humanlike was this cradling, intimate touch that we named it "the walrus hug."

Their incessant desire for tactile reassurance and their essential need for each other astonished us. It thoroughly contradicted the idea of the wicked brain-sucking walrus that we had been warned about. We realized in fact that if we could record the devotion walruses demonstrated, especially between mother and calf, then we could provide a familiar and powerfully emotional scene that would have mass appeal to audiences everywhere.

Even while we were captivated by these first encounters, I could never fully calm down underwater. Watching the walruses hug their companions reminded me of how strong they were and how dangerous they could be. The need for the cage only reinforced the fear. At the same time, I realized that if we were ever going to film the intimate details of a walrus's life, I would have to leave the cage and be able to relax in their realm.

Our First Encounter with a Polar Bear (told by Sarah Robertson)

While returning to the Arctic to focus on documenting the relationship between mother and baby walruses, we had an encounter that Adam and I will never forget. We were gripped by a primordial, adrenaline-fueled fear that only comes when face to face with a wild, predatory animal.

It was a beautiful summer day. Adam and I were standing on a small free-floating piece of ice, pointing our cameras at a herd of walruses that were floating not far off on their own chunk of ice. The hundred-member herd was full of small babies. The conditions were perfect. The wind and current were traveling in the same direction, pushing the ice herd directly toward us. Within minutes, their ice raft would be right up against ours. I was confident that we could get some terrific images.

However, the wind was also creating small waves, which were smashing our support boat against the ice. To avoid damage to the hull, it had to move. We had no walkie-talkies or radios. Before our guide steered the boat away, we took out everything that we thought we would need. The walruses were getting closer. We wanted the boat to leave fast so as not to disturb the herd.

As we waited, I grew concerned about how far the boat had drifted from us. Adam disregarded my concern. If we needed him to come, we would just wave. Besides, what could go wrong? And then it hit us. We had forgotten the one crucial piece of equipment on board the boat that we might need: our rifle.

Out of the corner of my eye, I saw the polar bear coming. "Nanook!" I whispered. It was the first polar bear I had ever seen in the wild. As the bear approached, I could see his hunger in the intense focus he held on the walruses. He was in full hunting mode, like a big cat with his ears back and body crouched low.

The walruses were oblivious to his approach, and the polar bear, totally focused on the herd, had not noticed us. Bears, said the science of the day, very rarely hunted walruses. And of those that did, it was only the large male bears that would dare try. Yet, right before our eyes was a young polar bear about to attack a herd of walruses. It was a wildlife cinematographer's dream. It can take decades to be in the right place at the right time for such a moment. And here we were, so fortunate to be set up with our cameras ready, only yards away from a battle about to take place between two Arctic giants.

There was one big problem. In order to get to the walrus herd, the bear had to pass right through our tiny piece of floating ice. Without a rifle or a guide to watch our backs, we felt excruciatingly vulnerable.

Should we sit quietly and try to film what was sure to be a one-of-a-kind dramatic event? Or should we shout to distract the bear? If we did shout, would we scare the bear away? Or would we focus the bear's attention on us? Would we become the hunted?

The racket and the stench of the walruses were getting closer. Soon a hundred panicked walruses would be right on top of us. Instinctively, we tripped the shutters and our cameras began rolling.

As the bear got closer, the herd's outer rim of female walruses started to stir. They could smell danger approaching and sounded the alarm with frantic barks. A thunder arose as the herd started to shift. Several thousand–pound animals slid into the water. A tidal

Two polar bears rest after a long crossing in the sea. The floe provides the bears with a ride to their next hunting grounds.

wave of ice water splashed up to our feet. The bear made his move and sprang forward. So did I. I shouted and waved my hands wildly, and Adam quickly joined in. Chaos erupted. The walruses piled into the water in groups, bellowing their surprise and anxiety. Each panicked walrus created waves of water. The swells rocked our tiny chunk of ice, threatening to capsize it and plunge us into the frigid water.

We continued madly waving our arms and yelling to alert our guide in the boat. The bear, fully aware of us now, stopped and looked at us in surprise. He sniffed the air, turned around, and walked away. The entire herd of walruses had disappeared underwater.

I sat down on the ice utterly dejected. Only seconds earlier, we had managed to position ourselves in one of the best situations a wildlife cinematographer could ever find. I had blown the chance of a lifetime. I realized how inexperienced we were. At that moment, my spirits were crushed, and I thought our careers were over.

This failure taught us a great lesson. That day we felt for the first time what it was like to be active participants in the events we wanted to photograph. Only feet away, we felt the intense drama of possibly meeting the Arctic's most ferocious beast, but we were totally unprepared to take part in the dynamic. We had no experience in either the physical or psychological preparation needed for such an encounter.

When we went home, we couldn't stop talking about the experience. How events converged and erupted in a sudden, unexpected drama. How the tension between the bear and the herd was palpable. How the sound of panicked walruses made the air tremble. This close-up, experimental photography was a different type of filmmaking. We were to learn that the Arctic required it. In the north, there are no man-made observation platforms, no safety vehicles to shoot from, no cabins, and no cliffside retreats. The only way to get shots was to be out on the ice with the animals and to be prepared. We hoped that this rare moment would happen again. And, next time, we would be ready.

A Second Chance (told by sarah robertson)

Later that year, we were back on the ice filming when a bear came into our midst to steal packets of walrus meat that had been butchered after an Inuit hunt. It was a ghost of a bear—suddenly standing before us on the ice ridge without warning. White on white, he was perfectly camouflaged and his instant presence shocked us.

Thoroughly unnerved, we stood our ground, cameras ready, and filmed the young bear's approach. An Inuit hunter shot near the bear's paws in an attempt to scare it away. The bear didn't even flinch, and he continued to advance. Everyone backed up to the edges of the ice. Our cameras kept rolling. The bear came within feet of us but passed right by, grabbed some walrus meat, and began eating.

As the bear gorged himself, the Inuit returned to their catch and recovered what they could of their hunt. They were dangerously close. With only five feet of ice between them, bear and man shared in what they both needed. They formed extraordinary images: Two species working out new relationships on a piece of floating ice miles out in the Arctic Ocean. Once again, we felt the excitement and thrill of the strange dynamics in the work that we were learning. In a small way, we began to redeem ourselves for our failure earlier in the year.

We learned much about polar bears from those two encounters that year. Both bears were young and hungry. Both took huge risks doing things that, more than likely, they had never done before. They were learning. They were trying out new initiatives, doing what they needed to do to survive. And we were learning, too.

The Stakeout (told by adam ravetch)

We decided to continue our work with walruses and bears. A large part of their lives was still unknown. We knew where to find them in the ice, but where did they go when the ice all but disappeared? So we set out to find them and to photograph them.

Since the year 2000, we have observed that the great walrus herds of northern Hudson Bay have been

Tourists stop for a photo in Foxe Basin, Canada. Nearly as big as the boat, a bull walrus lifts himself up to watch the intruders. FOLLOWING PAGE:
Sneaking in a shot from the sea, Adam Ravetch approaches a walrus from downwind. The walrus, not detecting his scent, continues to loaf sleepily.

congregating on remote, barren islands during a few summer weeks when there was no ice. Their need to get out of the water to rest brings together thousands of walruses on these rocky outposts. With this development in mind, I set up camp on a tiny island and tried to make myself as inconspicuous as possible. The island was the size of a football field, barely above sea level.

Since I was going to live with the walruses, I traveled to the island ahead of them to give myself time to set up. As the ice melted, the walruses came. Overnight, my island went from a population of one to a bustling, crowded walrus city with thousands of blubbery, barking walruses arriving and hauling out onto the rocks.

Here they would stay until the ice returned. But the time was brief. In only a few weeks the ice would be back and the walruses would leave. Now that there were walruses, I needed bears.

And so the waiting game began. Waiting around for a bear attack is never fun. It's some of the hardest work I've ever done. Every day I woke up at first light, sitting, watching, and waiting for 19 hours straight until the sun

went down. During the stakeout, I didn't move around very much, and I tried not to sleep. I spent all of my energy watching, waiting, and hoping that a bear would arrive. Days turned into weeks and, then, into months. Most people would call this an obsession, and I suppose it was. Yet my whole effort was to make sure that the cameras were rolling at the one crucial moment when a bear finally shows up and hunts. My greatest fear, always, was that I would miss the action.

A bear would usually arrive when the winds were strong, and the stench of a walrus herd wafted into the air currents. Over the years, I have come to know the walrus's distinct smell all too well, and it's not pleasant. But for a polar bear, it's like ringing a dinner bell. Polar bears can detect smells up to 40 miles away, maybe even farther. It was that sharp sense of smell that I was hoping would lead a bear right to me.

Once a bear does show, the tension rises. First there is always a meet-and-greet session. I couldn't avoid it. After that the negotiations started. Sometimes the agreement was reached quickly; other times I had to

elaborate by shouting, banging pots and pans, and shooting noisemakers into the air. I would try anything to make the bear understand that I was not there to harm him, or to compete with him for food. At the same time, the bear needed to realize that I required my own space, and I was not available for eating.

Sometimes the meet-and-greet would happen at night, when the bears had a distinct advantage. I named these bears the "Woofers," because of the sound they made when I awoke to the heavy breathing of a bear outside my tent. It is terrifying when a Woofer is smelling your face, inches away, in the pitch darkness. The fear of being hunted by a polar bear even penetrates my dreams to this day when I'm safe at home.

Bears are intensely curious and resourceful creatures. They have to be. If they have nothing to eat, then their curiosity drives them forward to investigate a strange object or smell on the horizon to find possible new food sources: a skinny man caught in a sleeping bag or a 2,000-pound packet of fat tied up in a tough, leathery hide will do. They do not discriminate.

When I first started these island stakeouts, it was just a single bear that would show. Bears normally eat ringed seals that live in the ice. Now, with ice-free seasons increasing every year in the Arctic, more and more bears are driven to these remote islands. It's very difficult to hunt a seal in the open water. But a walrus, marooned on land, even though it's armed with a pair of two-foot, daggerlike tusks, is a real possibility.

So picture this: a windswept, fog-bound football-field of an island with a tiny tent perched in the middle. Thousands of walruses are hauled out on the shores to the left of me. Five bears are lounging in the sand on the shores to the right of me. There we were, three species living side by side in a highly unusual circumstance. Never in my life had I felt so alive.

The walruses knew that the bears were there, but there was nowhere to hide, so they employed the herding strategy: safety in numbers. Laying their heads inward and their bodies outward, the walruses systematically piled their bodies on top of each other, forming an impenetrable wall of blubber. So closely packed were the walruses that the heat of their bodies produced a steam cloud hovering over the herd like an umbrella, and sometimes it engulfed them in a wall of fog. The need for walruses to touch each other had never been so evident. Flipper touching flipper, the walruses can sleep, even with bears about. Should a walrus become startled, then, like a line of dominoes, they all feel the shift and leap up to the ready.

BATTLE OF GIANTS (TOLD BY ADAM RAVETCH)

What makes a bear that has been sleeping for weeks finally decide to hunt? I'll never know, but I was up at four in the morning with my camera ready. The walruses were in their usual sleep formation.

In the water I saw what looked like a seagull swimming toward the herd. Checking it out through my camera lens, I saw that it was the head of a swimming polar bear. I had to contain my excitement. I had been waiting for weeks for this one moment. The adrenaline began to pump and my hands were shaking.

In an instant, the bear charged out of the water and plunged into the walrus herd. The walruses panicked and went straight for the sea. Barking, undulating red and brown bodies stabbed at the bear as they ran for the water. The bear bobbed and weaved through the gauntlet of daggers. In the confusion, a small walrus calf became exposed. The bear leapt and grabbed it in its mouth. I thought the calf was finished, but, to my amazement, a female walrus climbed back up the rocks intent on confronting the bear. With incredible agility, this 2,000-pound animal hoisted herself up to the bear and attacked him with her tusks. Her quick, valiant decision saved the young walrus's life, yet left her mortally wounded. The bear exhausted the large walrus, immobilizing it and in the end suffocating it.

Sitting on the beach after documenting this rare behavior, I was filled with amazement at the courage this female had exhibited. The sacrifice of her life for

Filmmaker Adam Ravetch wears his dry suit, always ready to go in the water at any time. Here, he is setting up to film a herd near Igloolik, Canada.
OPPOSITE: *A bull walrus basks in the sun. His skin turns red as the increasing blood flow helps release some of his body heat, cooling him off.*

the betterment of the herd was so humanlike. Finally, I was overtaken by exhaustion. I slept for three days.

I have returned to the island almost every year since that first stakeout. When Sarah and I first started filming in the Arctic, bear attacks on walruses was considered to be very rare. Now, this event not only occurs more regularly, but I see certain polar bears hunting and eating walruses every year.

At the end of the last summer of filming, I was back on my island in the Arctic, well into October. I called for a boat on the mainland to come get me to return home. Getting off the island used to be a precarious maneuver because of the ice that always surrounded it. I had often been stuck for unplanned days and weeks, waiting for the ice to shift. This year, there had been no ice since June, and I was easily plucked off the island. Before I headed home, I circled the island to take some last film of the bears and walruses. Already they had spent four months as refugees on this rock.

I hoped I wasn't witnessing the only option left for walruses and bears, forever stuck on a small rock outcropping. As our boat turned away from the island, all of them seemed to be looking out toward the sea, longing for the smell of the returning cold and ice.

Making *Arctic Tale* has been about a lot more than just chasing the adventure of a monster. It's about telling the stories of a place we love and want to protect. With the Arctic warming twice as fast as anywhere else on our planet, we feel as if a new phase of our work is just beginning. Our cameras must continue to point north. Up to now, we have seen the capability, the intelligence, and the resourcefulness of bears and walruses, but how will their lives continue to play out and evolve as they respond to the dramatic changes in their world?

FOLLOWING PAGES: *Stranded on an outcrop of rock, a polar bear waits for the ice to return. Each summer, bears come ashore on Baffin Island after the pack ice melts, sometimes spending up to four months on land.*

ACKNOWLEDGMENTS

National Geographic wishes to thank Adam Ravetch, Sarah Robertson, Adam Leipzig, Tim Kelly, Will Weil, and Kattie Evans for their help in adapting the *Arctic Tale* story and screenplay, and Donnali Fifield for all of her hard work on the text. In addition we would like to thank the knowledgeable staff of the National Geographic Image Collection, especially Stacy Gold and Paula Soderlund for their invaluable assistance researching images to accompany the text. Expert consultants Becky Sjare and Scott Schliebe, and indefatigable researcher Meaghan Mulholland carefully reviewed the text. Aileen Robertson, Agnes Tabah, and Bernice Chu were essential to this project, as were copyeditors Erica Rose and Jane Sunderland.

ILLUSTRATIONS CREDITS

4-5, Norbert Rosing/NG Image Collection; 6-7, Paul Nicklen/NG Image Collection; 8-9, Ira Block/NG Image Collection; 10-11, Joel Sartore; 12, Markus Moellenberg/CORBIS; 14-15, David McLain; 16, Paul Nicklen/NG Image Collection; 17, Norbert Rosing/NG Image Collection; 18-19, Paul Nicklen/NG Image Collection; 20, Norbert Rosing/NG Image Collection; 21, Norbert Rosing; 22-23, David McLain; 24, Paul Nicklen/NG Image Collection; 25 (UP LE), Norbert Rosing/NG Image Collection; 25 (UP RT), Norbert Rosing/NG Image Collection; 25 (CTR LE), Norbert Rosing/NG Image Collection; 25 (CTR RT), Norbert Rosing/NG Image Collection; 25 (LO LE), Norbert Rosing/NG Image Collection; 25 (LO RT), Norbert Rosing/NG Image Collection; 26, Norbert Rosing/NG Image Collection; 27, Norbert Rosing/NG Image Collection; 28-29, Norbert Rosing/NG Image Collection; 30, Paul Nicklen/NG Image Collection; 31, Norbert Rosing/NG Image Collection; 32 (UP), Norbert Rosing/NG Image Collection; 32 (LO), Norbert Rosing/NG Image Collection; 33, Amos Nachoum; 34-35, Richard Olsenius/NG Image Collection; 36, Paul Nicklen/NG Image Collection; 37, Norbert Rosing/NG Image Collection; 38, Norbert Rosing/NG Image Collection; 39 (UP), Norbert Rosing/NG Image Collection; 39 (CTR), Norbert Rosing/NG Image Collection; 39 (LO), Norbert Rosing/NG Image Collection; 40-41, Paul Nicklen/NG Image Collection; 42, Ralph Lee Hopkins/NG Image Collection; 43 (UP), Paul Nicklen/NG Image Collection; 43 (LO), Paul Nicklen/NG Image Collection; 44, Paul Nicklen/NG Image Collection; 45, Paul Nicklen/NG Image Collection; 46, Norbert Rosing/NG Image Collection; 47, Paul Nicklen/NG Image Collection; 48-49, Paul Nicklen/NG Image Collection; 50, Nick Caloyianis/NG Image Collection; 51, Paul Nicklen/NG Image Collection; 52, Ralph Lee Hopkins/NG Image Collection; 53, Paul Nicklen/NG Image Collection; 54-55, Kennan Ward/CORBIS; 56, Paul Nicklen/NG Image Collection; 57, Paul Nicklen/NG Image Collection; 58, Göran Ehlmé; 59, Paul Nicklen/NG Image Collection; 60-61, John Dunn/Arctic Light/NG Image Collection; 62, Paul Nicklen/NG Image Collection; 63, Joel Sartore/NG Image Collection; 64, Paul Nicklen/NG Image Collection; 65 (UP), Bill Curtsinger/NG Image Collection; 65 (LO), Paul Nicklen/NG Image Collection; 66-67, George F. Mobley; 68, Karen Kasmauski/NG Image Collection; 69, Joel Sartore; 70, Paul Nicklen/NG Image Collection; 71, Paul Nicklen/NG Image Collection; 72-73, Paul Nicklen/NG Image Collection; 74, Ralph Lee Hopkins/NG Image Collection; 75, Ralph Lee Hopkins/NG Image Collection; 76, Norbert Rosing; 77, Ralph Lee Hopkins/NG Image Collection; 78-79, Norbert Rosing/NG Image Collection; 80, Bill Curtsinger/NG Image Collection; 81, Norbert Rosing/NG Image Collection; 82, Ralph Lee Hopkins/NG Image Collection; 83, Paul Nicklen/NG Image Collection; 84-85, Ralph Lee Hopkins/NG Image Collection; 86, Norbert Rosing/NG Image Collection; 87, Paul Nicklen/NG Image Collection; 88, Norbert Rosing/NG Image Collection; 89, Norbert Rosing/NG Image Collection; 90-91, John Dunn/NG Image Collection; 92, Paul Nicklen/NG Image Collection; 93, Paul Nicklen/NG Image Collection; 94-95, Robert Wallis/CORBIS; 96, Ralph Lee Hopkins/NG Image Collection; 97, Paul Nicklen/NG Image Collection; 98, Flip Nicklin/Minden Pictures; 99, Norbert Rosing/NG Image Collection; 100-101, Ralph Lee Hopkins/NG Image Collection; 102, Ralph Lee Hopkins/NG Image Collection; 103 (UP), Ralph Lee Hopkins/NG Image Collection; 103 (CTR), Ralph Lee Hopkins/NG Image Collection; 103 (LO), Ralph Lee Hopkins/NG Image Collection; 104-105, Norbert Rosing/NG Image Collection; 106, Paul Nicklen/NG Image Collection; 107, Norbert Rosing/NG Image Collection; 108, Flip Nicklin/Minden Pictures; 109, Joel Sartore; 110, Norbert Rosing/NG Image Collection; 111, Paul Nicklen/NG Image Collection; 112-113, Onne van der Wal/CORBIS; 114, Paul Nicklen/NG Image Collection; 115, Paul Nicklen/NG Image Collection; 116, Norbert Rosing/NG Image Collection; 117, Norbert Rosing/NG Image Collection; 118-119, David Keaton/CORBIS; 120, Paul Nicklen/NG Image Collection; 121, Paul Nicklen/NG Image Collection; 122, Norbert Rosing/NG Image Collection; 123, Matthias Breiter/Minden Pictures; 124, Ralph Lee Hopkins/NG Image Collection; 125, Norbert Rosing/NG Image Collection; 126-127, Paul Nicklen/NG Image Collection; 128, Paul Nicklen/NG Image Collection; 129 (UP), Paul Nicklen/NG Image Collection; 129 (LO), Paul Nicklen/NG Image Collection; 130, Paul Nicklen/NG Image Collection; 131, Paul Nicklen/NG Image Collection; 132-133, Paul Nicklen/NG Image Collection; 134, Paul Nicklen/NG Image Collection; 135, Paul Nicklen/NG Image Collection; 136, Paul Nicklen/NG Image Collection; 137, Paul Nicklen/NG Image Collection; 138-139, George F. Mobley; 140, Emory Kristof/Kevin Raskoff/Chris Nicholson; 141, Brian Skerry; 142 (UP), Paul Nicklen/NG Image Collection; 142 (LO), Norbert Rosing/NG Image Collection; 143, John Dunn/Arctic Light/NG Image Collection; 144, Paul Nicklen/NG Image Collection; 146, Nick Caloyianis; 147 (UP), Alain Saint Hilaire; 147 (CTR), Sarah Robertson; 147 (LO), Paul Nicklen/NG Image Collection; 149, Paul Nicklen/NG Image Collection; 151, Paul Nicklen/NG Image Collection; 152, Amos Nachoum; 154, Amos Nachoum; 155, Paul Nicklen/NG Image Collection; 156-157, Paul Nicklen/NG Image Collection; 158, Paul Nicklen/NG Image Collection; 160, Paul Nicklen/NG Image Collection.

The floe edge, where the ice meets the open water, changes constantly as the ice melts and reforms. Beyond it, the Arctic Ocean stretches to the horizon.
FOLLOWING PAGE: *Polar bear tracks in the snow.*

ARCTIC TALE

Published by the National Geographic Society

John M. Fahey, Jr., *President and Chief Executive Officer*

Gilbert M. Grosvenor, *Chairman of the Board*

Nina D. Hoffman, *Executive Vice President;*
   President, Book Publishing Group

Prepared by the Book Division

Kevin Mulroy, *Senior Vice President and Publisher*

Leah Bendavid-Val, *Director of Photography Publishing*
   and Illustrations

Marianne R. Koszorus, *Director of Design*

Barbara Brownell Grogan, *Executive Editor*

Elizabeth Newhouse, *Director of Travel Publishing*

Staff for this Book

Lisa Thomas, *Project Editor*

Donnali Fifield, *Writer*

Adam Ravetch, Sarah Robertson, *Contributing Writers*

Becky Sjare, Scott Schliebe, *Editorial Consultants*

Meaghan Mulholland, *Researcher*

Peggy Archambault, *Art Director*

Sanaa Akkach, *Designer*

Meredith Wilcox, *Administrative Director of Illustrations*

Dana Chivvis, *Illustrations Editor*

Stacy Gold, Paula Soderlund, *Illustrations Research*

Marshall Kiker, *Illustrations Specialist*

Jennifer Thornton, *Managing Editor*

Gary Colbert, *Production Director*

Richard Wain, *Production Manager*

Manufacturing and Quality Management

Christopher A. Liedel, *Chief Financial Officer*

Phillip L. Schlosser, *Vice President*

John T. Dunn, *Technical Director*

Chris Brown, *Director*

Maryclare Tracy, *Manager*

Nicole Elliott, *Manager*